Cute Croch... for Girls™

Leslie Coggin
Crocheted Creations
205 643-6898

MW00637903

Contents

Hearts *Aplenty*

SKILL LEVEL

INTERMEDIATE

FINISHED SIZES

Dress: Instructions given fit girl's size 2; changes for sizes 3, 4, 5 and 6 are in [ ]·

Kerchief: 11 inches wide x 11 inches long

FINISHED GARMENT SIZES

Chest: 22inches (*size 2*) [23 inches (*size 3*), 23½ inches (*size 4*), 24¼ inches (*size 5*), 25 inches (*size 6*)]

MATERIALS

- Caron Spa light (light worsted) weight yarn (3 oz/251 yds/85g per skein)
  2 [2, 3, 3, 3] skeins #0007 naturally
  1 skein each for all sizes #0005 ocean spray, #0010 stormy blue, #0008 misty taupe
- Aunt Lydia's Bamboo Crochet Thread size 10 (300 yds per ball)
  1 ball for all sizes #1 white
- Size G/6/4mm crochet hook or size needed to obtain gauge
- Size 6/1.80mm steel crochet hook
- Tapestry needle

GAUGE

20 sc = 4 inches

PATTERN NOTES

Weave in ends as work progresses.

Join with slip stitch as indicated unless otherwise stated.

Chain-4 at beginning of row counts as first treble crochet unless otherwise stated.

SPECIAL STITCHES

Shell: 5 dc in st indicated.

Beginning shell (beg shell): Ch 3, 4 dc in st indicated.

INSTRUCTIONS
DRESS
FRONT
FIRST HEART
Rnd 1 (RS): With size G hook and ocean spray, ch 2, 10 hdc in 2nd ch from hook, **join** (see Pattern Notes) in first hdc. (10 hdc)

Rnd 2: Ch 3, 2 tr in same hdc as joining, (tr, dc) in next hdc (mark last tr made for joining of yoke), 2 hdc in next hdc, hdc in next hdc, sc in next hdc, ch 3, sl st in 3rd ch from hook (picot made), sc in next hdc, hdc in next hdc, 2 hdc in next hdc, (dc, tr) in next hdc (mark last tr made for joining of next heart), (2 tr, ch 3, sl st) in next hdc. Fasten off. (6 tr, 2 dc, 6 hdc, 2 sc, 2 ch-3 sps)

2ND HEART
Rnd 1: With stormy blue, rep rnd 1 of First Heart.

Rnd 2: Ch 3, 2 tr in same hdc, tr in next hdc, sl st in marked st on RS of last heart, on working heart, dc in same st as last tr made, 2 hdc in next hdc, hdc in next hdc, sc in next hdc, picot, sc in next hdc, hdc in next hdc, 2 hdc in next hdc, (dc, tr) in next hdc (mark last tr made for joining of next heart), (2 tr, ch 3, sl st) in next hdc. Fasten off.

3RD HEART
With misty taupe, work same as 2nd Heart. Do not mark tr on last rnd.

YOKE
Row 1 (RS): With size G hook, join naturally in marked tr on First Heart marked for yoke joining, **ch 4** (see Pattern Notes), 2 tr in same tr as joining, tr in next dc, dc in next hdc, hdc in each of next 2 hdc, sc in next sc, sc in next picot, [ch 9, sc in picot at bottom of next heart] twice, working across next side, sc in next sc, hdc in each of next 2 hdc, dc in next hdc, tr in next dc, 3 tr in next tr, turn. (8 tr, 2 dc, 4 hdc, 5 sc, 2 ch-9 sps)

Row 2: Ch 4, tr in first tr, tr in next st, dc in next st, hdc in each of next 2 sts, sc in each of next 4 sts, 9 sc in next ch-9 sp, sc in next sc, 9 sc in next ch-9 sp, sc in each of next 4 sts, hdc in each of next 2 sts, dc in next st, tr in next st, 2 tr in 4th ch of beg ch-4, turn. (6 tr, 2 dc, 4 hdc, 27 sc)

Row 3: Ch 2, sc in 2nd ch from hook, sc in each st across to last st, 2 sc in last st, turn. (41 sts)

Rows 4–6 (4–7, 4–8, 4–9, 4–10): Rep row 3. (47 [49, 51, 53, 55] sc at end of last row)

SIZES 2, 4, 6
Row 7 [9, 11]: Ch 1, sc in each sc across. Fasten off.

SIZES 3 & 5
Fasten off.

BACK
Work same as Front. At end of last row, do not fasten off.

JOINING FRONT & BACK
Rnd 1 (WS): Ch 1, sc in each sc across, ch 8 (underarm made), hold Front with WS facing, sc in each sc of Front, ch 8 (underarm made), join in first sc, turn. (94 [98, 102, 106, 110] sc, 2 ch-8 sps)

Rnd 2 (RS): Ch 1, sc in each of first 8 chs, sc in each of next 47 [49, 51, 53, 55] sc, sc in each of next 8 chs sc in each of next 47 [49, 51, 53, 55] sc, join in first sc. Do not turn. (110 [114, 118, 122, 126] sc)

SKIRT
Rnd 1: Ch 4, tr in same st, tr in each of next 54 [56, 58, 60, 62] sc, 2 tr in next sc, tr in each of next 54 [56, 58, 60, 62] sc, join in 4th ch of beg ch-4. (112 [116, 120, 124, 128] tr)

Rnd 2: Ch 1, (sc, ch 2, sc) in same tr, sk next tr, *(sc, ch 2, sc) in next tr, sk next tr, rep from * around, join in first sc. (112, [116, 120, 124, 128] sc, 56 [58, 60, 62, 64] ch-2 sps)

Rnd 3: Ch 1, sc in first ch-2 sp, **shell** (see Special Stitches) in next ch-2 sp, *sc in next ch-2 sp, shell in next ch-2 sp, rep from * around, join in first sc. (28 [29, 30, 31, 32] shells, 28 [29, 30, 31, 32] sc)

Rnd 4: Ch 1, (sc, ch 2, sc) in same sc, sk next 2 dc, (sc, ch 2, sc) in next dc, sk next 2 dc, *(sc, ch 2, sc) in next sc, sk next 2 dc, (sc, ch 2, sc) in next dc, sk next 2 sc, rep from * around, join in first sc. (112 [116, 120, 124, 128] sc, 56 [58, 60, 62, 64] ch-2 sps)

Rnd 5: Sl st in first ch-2 sp, **beg shell** (*see Special Stitches*) in same ch-2 sp, sc in next ch-2 sp, *shell in next ch-2 sp, sc in next ch-2 sp, rep from * around, join in 3rd ch of beg ch-3. (*28 [29, 30, 31, 32] shells, 28 [29, 30, 31, 32] sc*)

Rnd 6: Sl st in each of next 2 dc, ch 1, (sc, ch 2, sc) in same dc, sk next 2 dc, (sc, ch 2, sc) in next sc, *sk next 2 dc, (sc, ch 2, sc) in next dc, sk next 2 dc, (sc, ch 2, sc) in next sc, rep from * around, join in first sc. (*112 [116, 120, 124, 128] sc, 56 [58, 60, 62, 64] ch-2 sps*)

Rnd 7: Rep rnd 3.

Rnd 8: Ch 1, (sc, ch 2, sc) in same sc, sk next 2 dc, (sc, ch 2, sc) in next dc, sk next 2 dc, *(sc, ch 2, sc) in next sc, sk next 2 dc, (sc, ch 2, sc) in next dc, sk next 2 dc, rep from * around, working (sc, ch 2, sc, ch 2, sc) in each of next 2 ch-2 sps at each side, join in first sc. (*116 [120, 124, 128, 132] sc, 60 [62, 64, 66, 68] ch-2 sps*)

Rnd 9: Rep rnd 5. (*30 [31, 32, 33, 34] shells, 30 [31, 32, 33, 34] sc at end of rnd*)

Rnd 10: Rep rnd 6. (*116 [120, 124, 128, 132] sc, 60 [62, 64, 66, 68] ch-2 sps*)

Rnd 11: Rep rnd 3. (*30 [31, 32, 33, 34] shells, 30 [31, 32, 33, 34] sc at end of rnd*)

Rnd 12: Rep rnd 4. (*116 [120, 124, 128, 132] sc, 60 [62, 64, 66, 68] ch-2 sps*)

Rnd 13: Rep rnd 5. (*30 [31, 32, 33, 34] shells, 30 [31, 32, 33, 34] sc at end of rnd*)

Rnd 14: Rep rnd 6, working (sc, ch 2, sc, ch 2, sc) in each of next 2 ch-2 sps at each side, join in first sc. (*120 [124, 128, 132, 136] sc, 64 [66, 68, 70, 72] ch-2 sps*)

Rep rnds 3–6 until piece measures approximately 7½ [8, 8½, 9, 9½] inches from rnd 1 of Body, ending with rnd 5.

FIRST RUFFLE

Rnd 1: Ch 1, (sc, ch 2, sc, ch 5, sc) in same sc (*mark ch-5 sp*), sk next 2 dc, (sc, ch 2, sc, ch 5, sc) in next dc, sk next 2 dc, *(sc, ch 2, sc, ch 5, sc) in next sc, sk next 2 dc, (sc, ch 2, sc, ch 5, sc) in next dc, sk next 2 dc, rep from * around, join in first sc.

Rnd 2: Sl st in next ch-2 sp, beg shell in same sp, sk next ch-5 sp, pushing sk ch-5 sp to WS, sc in next ch-2 sp, sk next ch-5 sp, *pushing sk ch-5 sp to WS, shell in next ch-2 sp, sk next ch-5 sp, pushing sk ch-5 sp to WS, sc in next ch-2 sp, sk next ch-5 sp, rep from * around, pushing last sk ch-5 sp to WS, join in 3rd ch of beg ch-3. Fasten off.

2ND RUFFLE

Rnd 1: Hold piece with RS facing, working in back of rnd 1 of First Ruffle and with size G hook, join ocean spray in marked ch-5 sp, ch 1, (sc, ch 2, sc, ch 5, sc) in same sp (*mark ch-5 sp*), (sc, ch 2, sc, ch 5, sc) in each ch-5 sp around, join in first sc.

Rnd 2: Sl st in first ch-2 sp, ch 1, (sc, ch 2, sc) in same sp, sk next ch-5 sp, working in front of sk ch-5 sp, (sc, ch 2, sc) in next ch-2 sp, sk next ch-5 sp, *working in front of sk ch-5 sp, (sc, ch 2, sc) in next ch-2 sp, sk next ch-5 sp, rep from * around, working in front of last sk ch-5 sp, join in first sc.

Rnd 3: Sl st in first ch-2 sp, beg shell in same sp, sc in next ch-2 sp, *shell in next ch-2 sp, sc in next ch-2 sp, rep from * around, join in 3rd ch of beg ch-3. Fasten off.

3RD RUFFLE
With stormy blue, work same as 2nd Ruffle.

4TH RUFFLE

Rnd 1: With RS facing, working in back of 3rd Ruffle and with size G hook, join misty taupe in marked ch-5 sp, ch 1, (sc, ch 2, sc) in same sp, (sc, ch 2, sc) in each rem ch-5 sp around, join in first sc.

Rnd 2: Rep rnd 3 of 2nd Ruffle.

UNDERARM EDGING
Hold piece with RS of 1 underarm section facing, join MC in marked ch from row 1 of Yoke, ch 1, working across next side in ends of rows, work 12 [13, 14, 15, 16] sc evenly sp down to unused lps of underarm, sc in each of next 8 unused lps, working across next side in ends of rows, work 12 [13, 14, 15, 16] sc evenly sp across to Heart. Fasten off. (*32 [34, 36, 38, 40] sc*)

Rep on other underarm.

TOP TRIM & TIES

Rnd 1: Hold piece with RS facing, with size 6 hook, join crochet thread in first tr on First Heart above yoke, ch 1, *working in chs and sts, work 15 sc evenly sp to center of Heart, sl st in stitching at edge of center crevice of Heart, working in sts and chs across last half of same Heart, work 15 sc evenly sp across**, sl st in sp between last Heart and next Heart, rep from * twice, ending last rep at **, 2 sc in each sc around underarm to First Heart on other side (*mark first and last sc made between hearts for ties*), ***working in chs and sts, work 15 sc evenly sp to center of Heart, sl st in stitching at edge of center crevice of Heart, working in sts and chs across last half of same Heart, work 15 sc evenly sp across****, sl st in sp between last Heart and next Heart, rep from *** 3 times, ending last rep at ****, 2 sc in each sc around underarm (*mark first and last sc made between hearts for ties*), join in first sc.

Rnd 2: Ch 1, *sc in each sc across to next marked st, ch 121, sl st in 2nd ch from hook, sc in **back bump** (*see Stitch Guide*) of each ch across (*tie made*), rep from * 4 times, sc in each sc across, join in first sc. Fasten off.

KERCHIEF
FIRST HEART
Work same as First Heart of Dress without marking tr for yoke joining.

2ND HEART
Work same as 2nd Heart of Dress.

3RD HEART
With misty taupe, work same as 2nd Heart of Dress.

4TH HEART
With stormy blue, work same as 2nd Heart of Dress.

5TH HEART
With ocean spray, work same as 2nd Heart of Dress. Do not mark tr on last rnd.

BODY
Foundation row: With RS of Hearts facing and with size G hook, join naturally in picot of First Heart, ch 1, sc in same picot, [ch 11, sc in picot of next heart] 4 times, turn. (5 sc, 4 ch-11 sps)

Row 1: Ch 1, sc in first sc, [ch 4, sk next 2 chs, sc in next ch] 3 times, *ch 4, sk next 2 chs, sc in next sc, [ch 4, sk next 2 chs, sc in next ch] 3 times, rep from * 2 times, ch 2, dc in last sc (ch 2 and dc counts as ch-4 sp). (16 ch-4 sps)

Row 2: Ch 1, (sc, ch 4, sc) in same sp, *ch 4, sc in next ch-4 sp, rep from * across to last ch-4 sp, ch 2, dc in last ch-4 sp (ch 2 and dc counts as ch-4 sp), turn. (16 ch-4 sps)

Row 3: Ch 1, sc in same sp, *ch 4, sc in next ch-4 sp, rep from * across to last ch-4 sp, ch 2, dc in last ch-4 sp, turn. (15 ch-4 sps)

Row 4: Ch 1, sc in same sp, ch 4, *sc in next ch-4 sp, ch 4, rep from * across to last ch-4 sp, (sc, ch 2, dc) in last ch-4 sp.

Row 5: Rep row 3. (14 ch-4 sps)

Rows 6–25: [Rep rows 2–5] five times. (4 ch-4 sps at end of last row)

Rows 26 & 27: Rep row 3. (2 ch-4 sps at end of last row)

Row 28: Ch 1, sc in same sp, ch 4, sc in next ch-4 sp. Fasten off. (1 ch-4 sp)

EDGING
Hold piece with RS facing, with size 6 hook, join crochet thread in last ch-4 sp of body, ch 1, 5 sc in same sp, working across next side in ends of rows, work 4 sc in each row across to First Heart, working across side of Heart: 2 sc in first sc, 2 sc in each of next 3 hdc, 2 sc in next dc, 2 sc in each of next 2 tr, ch 101, sl st in back bump of 2nd ch from hook and in each ch across (tie made), working across same Heart, sc in same tr that last 2 sc made, 3 sc in next tr, 3 sc in next ch, 2 sc in next ch, sl st in center crevice of Heart, 2 sc in each of next 2 chs, 3 sc in next ch, 3 sc in next tr, 2 sc in each of next 2 tr, sl st in sp between Heart and next Heart, work sc evenly sp around each rem Heart, working sl st in crevice of each Heart and in sp between Hearts, and working tie on side of last Heart, working across next side in ends of rows, 4 sc in each row across to first sc, join in first sc. Fasten off. ∎

Olivia Rose Set

SKILL LEVEL

INTERMEDIATE

FINISHED SIZES

Dress: Instructions given fit girl's size 2; changes for sizes 3, 4, 5 and 6 are in [ ].

Hat: Instructions given fit 18–19½ inches [19–20½ inches, 20–21½ inches]

FINISHED GARMENT SIZES

Chest: 22 inches *(size 2)* [23 inches *(size 3)*, 24 inches *(size 4)*, 25 inches *(size 5)*, 26 inches *(size 6)*]

Hat: 18 inches [19 inches, 20 inches]

MATERIALS

- Caron Joy! (2½ oz/138 yds/70.8g per skein)
  5 [5, 6, 6, 6] skeins #0001 snow
  1 skein each for all sizes #0002 cerise and #0004 kiwi
- Size H/8/5mm crochet hook or size needed to obtain gauge
- Tapestry needle
- Sewing needle
- 4 yds ⅝-inch-wide ribbon
- 2 yds ⅜-inch-wide ribbon
- White sewing thread

GAUGE

15 sc = 4 inches

PATTERN NOTES

Weave in ends as work progresses.

Join with slip stitch as indicated unless otherwise stated.

Chain-3 at beginning of round counts as first double crochet unless otherwise stated.

Chain-4 at beginning of round counts as first double crochet and chain-1 space unless otherwise stated.

SPECIAL STITCHES

Increase (inc): 2 dc in st.

Cluster (cl): Holding back last lp of each tr, 2 tr in st indicated, yo and draw through all 3 lps on hook.

INSTRUCTIONS
DRESS
BODICE
Rnd 1 (WS): Starting at underarm with snow, ch 82 [86, 90, 94, 98], being careful not to twist ch, **join** (see Pattern Notes) in first ch to form ring, ch 1, sc in each ch around, join in first sc, turn. (82 [86, 90, 94, 98] sc)

Rnd 2 (RS): Ch 1, sc in each sc around, join in first sc, turn.

Rnds 3–8 [3–8, 3–10, 3–10, 3–10]: Rep rnd 2. At end of last rnd, **do not turn.**

SKIRT
Rnd 1: **Ch 3** (see Pattern Notes), dc in each st around, working 8 [4, 10, 6, 12] **inc** (see Special Stitches) evenly sp around, join in 3rd ch of beg ch-3. (90 [90, 100, 100, 110] dc)

Rnd 2: Ch 1, **fpdc** (see Stitch Guide) around same ch as joining, sk next dc, [(sc, ch 2, sc) in next dc, sk next dc] 4 times, *fpdc around next dc, sk next dc, [(sc, ch 2, sc) in next dc, sk next dc] 4 times, rep from * around, join in first fpdc. (9 [9, 10, 10, 11] fpdc, 72 [72, 80, 80, 88] sc, 36 [36, 40, 40, 44] ch-2 sps)

Rnd 3: Ch 1, fpdc around same fpdc as joining, (sc, ch 2, sc) in each of next 4 ch-2 sps, *fpdc around next fpdc, (sc, ch 2, sc) in each of next 4 ch-2 sps, rep from * around, join in first fpdc.

Rnds 4–6: Rep rnd 3.

FIRST INCREASE SECTION
Rnd 1: Ch 1, fpdc around same fpdc as joining, (sc, ch 2, sc, ch 2, sc) in next ch-2 sp, (sc, ch 2, sc) in each of next 3 ch-2 sps, *fpdc around next fpdc, (sc, ch 2, sc, ch 2, sc) in next ch-2 sp, (sc, ch 2, sc) in each of next 3 ch-2 sps, rep from * around, join in first fpdc. (9 [9, 10, 10, 11] fpdc, 81 [81, 90, 90, 99] sc, 45 [45, 50, 50, 55] ch-2 sps)

Rnd 2: Ch 1, fpdc around same fpdc, (sc, ch 2, sc) in each of next 5 ch-2 sps, *fpdc around next fpdc, (sc, ch 2, sc) in each of next 5 ch-2 sps, rep from * around, join in first fpdc.

Rep rnd 2 until piece measures 6½ [6½, 6¾, 7, 7¼] inches from beg.

2ND INCREASE SECTION
Rnd 1: Ch 1, fpdc around same fpdc as joining, (sc, ch 2, sc, ch 2, sc) in next ch-2 sp, (sc, ch 2, sc) in each of next 4 ch-2 sps, *fpdc around next fpdc, (sc, ch 2, sc, ch 2, sc) in next ch-2 sp, (sc, ch 2, sc) in each of next 4 ch-2 sps, rep from * around, join in first fpdc. (9 [9, 10, 10, 11] fpdc, 99 [99, 110, 110, 121] sc, 54 [54, 60, 60, 66] ch-2 sps)

Rnd 2: Ch 1, fpdc around same fpdc as joining, (sc, ch 2, sc) in each of next 6 ch-2 sps, *fpdc around next fpdc, (sc, ch 2, sc) in each of next 6 ch-2 sps, rep from * around, join in first fpdc.

Rep rnd 2 until piece measures 10 [10, 10½, 11, 11½] inches from beg.

3RD INCREASE SECTION
Rnd 1: Ch 1, fpdc around same fpdc as joining, (sc, ch 2, sc, ch 2, sc) in next ch-2 sp, (sc, ch 2, sc) in each of next 5 ch-2 sps, *fpdc around next fpdc, (sc, ch 2, sc, ch 2, sc) in next ch-2 sp, (sc, ch 2, sc) in each of next 5 ch-2 sps, rep from * around, join in first fpdc. (9 [9, 10, 10, 11] fpdc, 117 [117, 130, 130, 143] sc, 63 [63, 70, 70, 77] ch-2 sps)

Rnd 2: Ch 1, fpdc around same fpdc as joining, (sc, ch 2, sc) in each of next 7 ch-2 sps, *fpdc around next fpdc, (sc, ch 2, sc) in each of next 7 ch-2 sps, rep from * around, join in first fpdc.

Rep rnd 2 until piece measures 14¾ [15¼, 15½, 16, 17] inches from beg.

EDGING
Rnd 1: Ch 1, fpdc around same fpdc as joining, sk next ch-2 sp, [**cl** (see Special Stitches) in next ch-2 sp, ch 4] twice, cl in same sp (flower made), sk next 3 ch-2 sps, [cl in next ch-2 sp, ch 4] twice, cl in same sp (flower made), sk next ch-2 sp, *fpdc around next fpdc, sk next ch-2 sp, [cl in next ch-2 sp, ch 4] twice, cl in same sp (flower made), sk next 3 ch-2 sps, [cl in next ch-2 sp, ch 4] twice, cl in same sp (flower made), sk next ch-2 sp, rep from * around, join in first fpdc. (18 [20, 20, 22, 22] flowers)

Rnd 2: Ch 1, fpdc around same fpdc as joining, 4 sc in each of next 2 ch-4 sps, sc in sp between last cl of last flower and first cl of next flower, 4 sc in each of next 2 ch-4 sps, *fpdc around next fpdc, 4 sc in each of next 2 ch-4 sps, sc in sp between last cl of last flower and first cl of next flower, 4 sc in each of next 2 ch-4 sps, rep from * around, join in first fpdc. (153 [153, 170, 170, 187] sc)

Rnd 3: Ch 1, fpdc around same fpdc as joining, sc in each of next 17 sc, *fpdc around next fpdc, sc in each of next 17 sc, rep from * around, join in first fpdc.

Rnd 4: Ch 1, fpdc around same fpdc as joining, dc in each of next 17 sc, *fpdc around next fpdc, dc in each of next 17 sc, rep from * around, join in first fpdc.

Rnd 5: Ch 1, fpdc around same fpdc as joining, sl st in next dc, [(sl st, ch 2, sl st) in next dc, sl st in next dc] 8 times, *fpdc around next fpdc, sl st in next dc, [(sl st, ch 2, sl st) in next dc, sl st in next dc] 8 times, rep from * around, join in first fpdc. Fasten off.

FRONT BODICE
Hold piece with RS facing and foundation ch at top, join snow in any unused lp of foundation ch.

Row 1: Ch 1, sc in same unused lp as joining, working in rem unused lps of foundation ch, sc in each of next 26 [27, 28, 29, 30] lps, leaving rem unused lps unworked, turn. (27 [28, 29, 30, 31] sc)

Row 2: Ch 1, **sc dec** (see Stitch Guide) in next 2 sc, sc in each sc across to last 2 sc, sc dec in last 2 sc, turn. (25 [26, 27, 28, 29] sc at end of last row)

Rows 3–8: Rep row 2. At end of last row, fasten off. (13 [14, 15, 16, 17] sc at end of last row)

BACK BODICE
Hold piece with RS facing, sk next 14 [15, 16, 17, 18] unused lps of foundation ch from Front Bodice, join snow in next unused lp. Work same as Front Bodice.

EDGING

Rnd 1: Hold piece with WS facing, join snow in first st in upper right corner of Back Bodice, ch 1, 3 sc in same sc, sc in each of next 11 [12, 13, 14, 15] sc, 3 sc in next st, working across side of bodice, sc in end of each of next 8 rows, sc in each of next 14 [15, 16, 17, 18] sts along underarm, working across next side of bodice, sc in end of each of next 8 rows, 3 sc in first sc of Front Bodice, sc in each of next 11 [12, 13, 14, 15] sc, 3 sc in next st, working across side of bodice, sc in end of each of next 8 rows, sc in each of next 14 [15, 16, 17, 18] sts along underarm, working across next side of bodice, sc in end of each of next 8 rows, join in first sc, turn. *(83 [86, 89, 92, 95] sc)*

Rnd 2: Ch 1, (sc, ch 2, sc) in same st, sl st in next st, *(sc, ch 2, sc) in next st, sk next st, sl st in next st, rep from * around, join in first sc. Fasten off. *(56 [58, 60 62, 64] sc, 56 [58, 60, 62, 62] sl sts, 28 [29, 30, 31, 32] ch-2 sps)*

FLOWER

Rnd 1 (RS): With snow, ch 5, **join** *(see Pattern Notes)* in 5th ch from hook to form ring, **ch 3** *(see Pattern Notes)*, 19 dc in ring, join in 3rd ch of beg ch-3. *(20 dc)*

Rnd 2: Ch 3, 3 dc in same ch as joining, 4 dc in each dc around, join in 3rd ch of beg ch-3, Leaving long end for sewing, fasten off. *(80 dc)*

LEAF COIL

With cerise, ch 22, 3 hdc in 2nd ch from hook and in each rem ch across. Fasten off.

FINISHING

Beg and ending at center back, weave ⅜-inch-wide ribbon through rnd 1 of Skirt going over 3 dc and under 2 dc. Sew Flower to center of Leaf Coil. Referring to photo for placement, sew Flower and Coil to front of Dress above rnd 1 of Skirt. Cut 4 pieces of 5/16-inch-wide ribbon, each 25 inches long. For each ribbon, fold end 1 inch twice and sew folded end to each corner on WS of Dress.

HAT

Rnd 1 (RS): With snow, ch 2, 14 [15, 16] hdc in 2nd ch from hook, join in first hdc. *(14 [15, 16] hdc)*

Rnd 2: Ch 1, fpdc around same hdc as joining, working behind fpdc just made, sc in top of same hdc, *fpdc around next hdc, working behind fpdc just made, sc in top of same hdc, rep from * around, join in first fpdc. *(14 [15, 16] fpdc, 14 [15, 16] sc)*

Rnd 3: Ch 1, fpdc around same fpdc as joining, sc in next sc, *fpdc around next fpdc, sc in next sc, rep from * around, join in first fpdc.

Rnd 4: Ch 1, fpdc around same fpdc as joining, (sc, ch 2, sc) in next sc, *fpdc around next fpdc, (sc, ch 2, sc) in next sc, rep from * around, join in first fpdc. *(14 [15, 16] fpdc, 28 [30, 32] sc, 14 [15, 16] ch-2 sps)*

Rnd 5: Ch 1, fpdc around same fpdc as joining, (sc, ch 2, sc) in next ch-2 sp, *fpdc around next fpdc, (sc, ch 2, sc) in next ch-2 sp, rep from * around, join in first fpdc.

Rnd 6: Ch 1, fpdc around same fpdc as joining, (sc, ch 2, sc, ch 2, sc) in next ch-2 sp, *fpdc around next fpdc, (sc, ch 2, sc, ch 2, sc) in next ch-2 sp, rep from * around, join in first fpdc. *(14 [15, 16] fpdc, 42 [45, 48] sc, 28 [30, 32] ch-2 sps)*

Rnd 7: Ch 1, fpdc around same fpdc as joining, (sc, ch 2, sc) in each of next 2 ch-2 sps, *fpdc around next fpdc, (sc, ch 2, sc) in each of next 2 ch-2 sps, rep from * around, join in first sc.

Rep rnd 7 until piece measures 5 [5¼, 5¼] inches from rnd 1 beg.

BRIM

Rnd 1: Sl st in next sc, **ch 4** *(see Pattern Notes)*, [tr in next sc, tr in next ch-2 sp, tr in next sc] twice, sk next fpdc, *[tr in next sc, tr in next ch-2 sp, tr in next sc] twice, sk next fpdc, rep from * around, join in 4th ch of beg ch-4. *(84 [90, 96] tr)*

Rnd 2: Ch 1, sc in each tr around, join in first sc.

Rnd 3: Ch 1, (sc, ch 2, sc) in same sc as joining, sk next sc, (sc, ch 2, sc, ch 2, sc) in next sc, sk next sc, (sc, ch 2, sc) in next sc, sk next sc, *(sc, ch 2, sc) in next sc, sk next sc, (sc, ch 2, sc, ch 2, sc) in next sc, sk next sc, (sc, ch 2, sc) in next sc, sk next sc, rep from * around, join in first sc. *(98 [108, 112] sc, 56 [60, 64] ch-2 sps)*

Rnd 4: Ch 1, (sc, ch 2, sc) in each ch-2 sp around, join in first sc. *(112 [120, 128] sc, 56 [60, 64] ch-2 sps)*

Rnds 5 & 6: Rep rnd 4.

Rnd 7: Ch 1, (sc, ch 2, sc) in first ch-2 sp, sk next ch-2 sp, [cl *(see Special Stitches)* in next ch-2 sp, ch 4] twice, cl in same sp *(flower made)*, sk next ch-2 sp, *(sc, ch 2, sc) in next ch-2 sp, sk next ch-2 sp, [cl in next ch-2 sp, ch 4] twice, cl in same sp *(flower made)*, sk next ch-2 sp, rep from * around, join in first sc. *(14 [15, 16] flowers, 56 [60, 64] sc, 28 [30, 32] ch-2 sps)*

Rnd 8: Ch 1, (sc, ch 2, sc) in first ch-2 sp, (sc, ch 2, sc, ch 2, sc) in each of next 2 ch-4 sps, *(sc, ch 2, sc) in next ch-2 sp, (sc, ch 2, sc, ch 2, sc) in each of next 2 ch-4 sps, rep from * around, join in first sc. Fasten off. *(98 [105, 112] ch-2 sps)*

FLOWER

Work same as Flower for Dress.

LEAF COIL

Work same as Leaf Coil for Dress.

FINISHING

Weave rem ⅝-inch-wide ribbon under post of any tr near post st on last rnd of Hat, *weave ribbon over next 5 tr and under next tr, rep from * around. Tie bow over last 5 sts. Trim ends. Sew Flower to center of Leaf Coil. Referring to photo for placement, sew Flower and Leaf Coil to brim on opposite side of Hat. ∎

Storytales Jumper & Tote

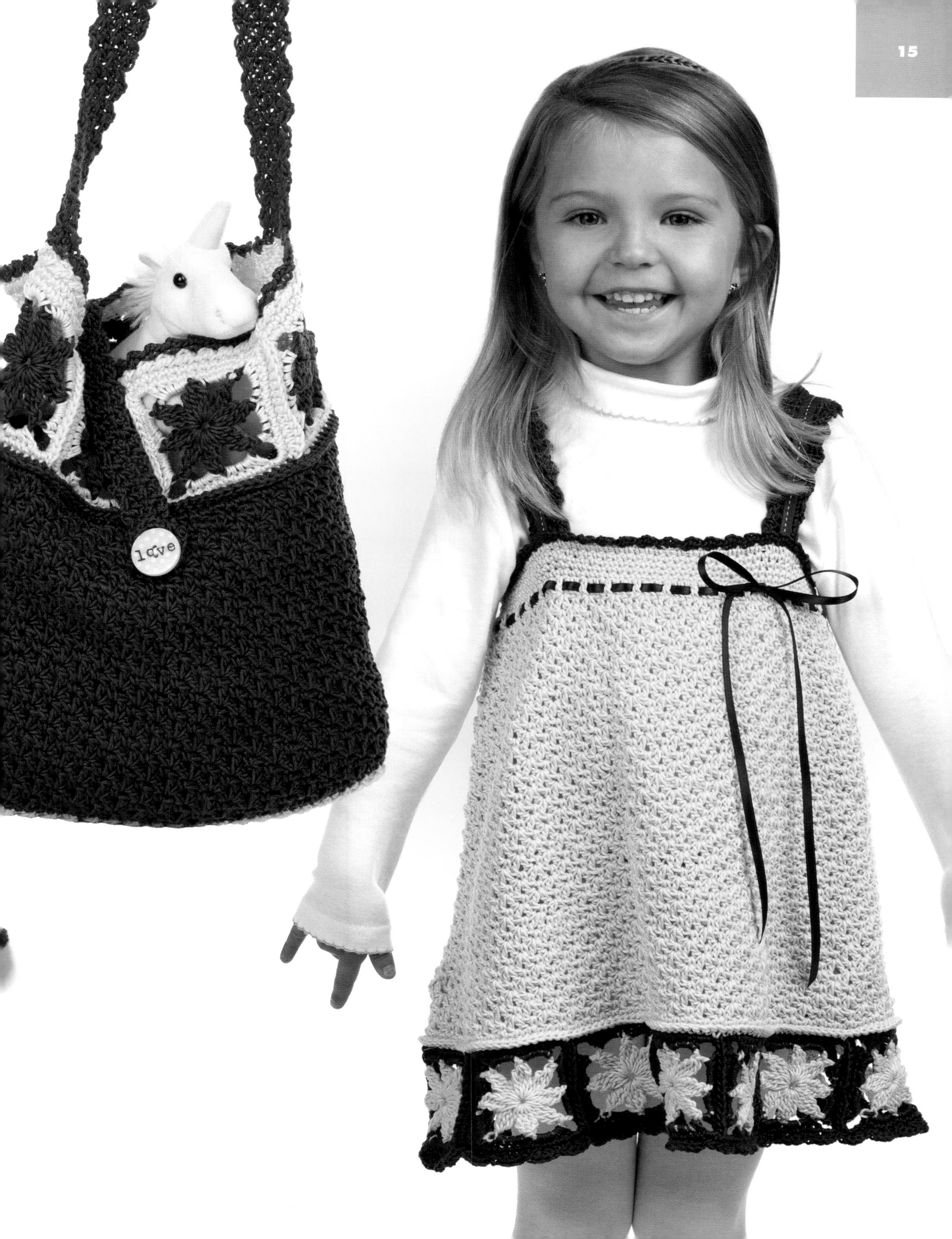
love

SKILL LEVEL

INTERMEDIATE

FINISHED SIZES

Dress: Instructions given fit girl's size 2; changes for sizes 3, 4, 5 and 6 are in [ ].
Tote: 11 inches x 13 inches x 2½ inches

FINISHED GARMENT SIZES

Chest: 22½ inches (*size 2*) [23½ inches (*size 3*), 24½ inches (*size 4*), 25½ inches (*size 5*), 26½ inches (*size 6*)]

MATERIALS

- Sinfonia sport weight cotton (3½ oz/ 232 yds/100g per skein)
  2 [3, 3, 4, 4] skeins #827 pink
  1 skein each for all sizes #838 brown
- Size F/5/3.75mm crochet hook or size needed to obtain gauge
- Tapestry needle
- Sewing needle
- 1 yd ⅛-inch-wide elastic
- 1½ yds ¼-inch-wide brown ribbon
- 1 yd ⅜-inch-wide brown ribbon
- 1-inch decorative button
- Matching sewing thread

GAUGE

16 sc = 4 inches

PATTERN NOTES

Weave in ends as work progresses.

Join with slip stitch as indicated unless otherwise stated.

Chain-3 at beginning of round counts as a double crochet unless otherwise stated.

Chain-4 at beginning of round counts as a double crochet and a chain-1 space unless otherwise stated.

SPECIAL STITCHES

V-st: (Dc, ch 1, dc) in st indicated.

Beginning V (beg V-st): (**Ch 4** (*see Pattern Notes*), dc) in st indicated.

Beginning cluster (beg cl): Ch 3, holding back last lp of each tr on hook, 2 tr in st indicated, yo and draw through all 3 lps on hook.

Cluster (cl): Holding back last lp of each tr on hook, 3 tr in st indicated, yo and draw through all 4 lps on hook.

Increase (inc): 2 dc in st.

INSTRUCTIONS
JUMPER
BORDER
FIRST MOTIF

Rnd 1 (RS): With pink, ch 5, **join** *(see Pattern Notes)* in 5th ch from hook to form ring, **beg cl** *(see Special Stitches)* in ring, ch 5, [**cl** *(see Special Stitches)* in ring, ch 5] 7 times, sk beg cl, join in 5th ch of next ch-5 sp. Change to brown by drawing lp through. Fasten off pink. *(8 cls, 8 ch-5 sps)*

Rnd 2: Ch 1, (hdc, 4 sc) in same ch-5 sp, (4 sc, hdc) in next ch-5 sp, ch 3, *(hdc, 4 sc) in next ch-5 sp, (4 sc, hdc) in next ch-5 sp, ch 3, rep from * twice, join in first hdc. *(8 hdc, 32 sc, 4 ch-3 sps)*

Rnd 3: Ch 1, sc in same hdc as joining, sc in each of next 9 sts, 5 sc in next ch-3 sp *(mark 2nd sc of last 5 sc made for joining of next motif)*, [sc in each of next 10 sts, 5 sc in next ch-3 sp] twice *(mark 2nd sc of last 5 sc made for joining of last motif)*, sc in each of next 10 sts, 5 sc in next ch-3 sp, join in first sc. Fasten off. *(60 sc)*

2ND MOTIF

Rnds 1 & 2: Rep rnds 1 and 2 of First Motif.

Rnd 3: Ch 1, sc in same hdc as joining, sc in each of next 9 sts, 3 sc in next ch-3 sp, holding First Motif with WS facing and working through both motifs **at same time**, sc in same ch-3 sp on working motif and in either marked sc on First Motif, sc in same ch-3 sp and in next sc on First Motif, sc in each of next 10 sts, [sc in next ch-3 sp and in next sc on First Motif] twice, on working motif only, 3 sc in same ch-3 sp, [sc in each of next 10 sts, 5 sc in next ch-3 sp] twice *(mark 2nd sc of last 5 sc made for joining of next motif)*, join in first sc. Fasten off.

3RD MOTIF

Rnds 1 & 2: Rep rnds 1 and 2 of First Motif.

Rnd 3: Ch 1, sc in same hdc as joining, sc in each of next 9 sts, 3 sc in next ch-3 sp, holding last completed motif with WS facing and working through both motifs **at same time**, sc in same ch-3 sp on working motif and in marked sc on last completed motif, sc in same ch-3 sp and in next sc on last completed motif, sc in each of next 10 sts, [sc in next ch-3 sp and in next sc on last completed motif] twice, on working motif only, 3 sc in same ch-3 sp, [sc in each of next 10 sts, 5 sc in next ch-3 sp] twice *(mark 2nd sc of last 5 sc made for joining of next motif)*, join in first sc. Fasten off.

4TH–10TH [4TH–11TH, 4TH–12TH, 4TH–13TH, 4TH–14TH] MOTIFS
Work same as 3rd Motif.

11TH [12TH, 13TH, 14TH, 15TH] MOTIF

Rnds 1 & 2: Rep rnds 1 and 2 of First Motif.

Rnd 3: Ch 1, sc in same hdc as joining, sc in each of next 9 sts, 3 sc in next ch-3 sp, holding last completed motif with WS facing and working through both motifs **at same time**, sc in same ch-3 sp on working motif and in marked sc on last completed motif, sc in same ch-3 sp and in next sc on last completed motif, sc in each of next 10 sts, [sc in next ch-3 sp and in next sc on last completed motif] twice, on working motif only, 3 sc in same ch-3 sp, sc in each of next 10 sts, 3 sc in next ch-3 sp, holding WS of First Motif facing and working through both motifs **at same time**, sc in same ch-3 sp and in marked sc on First Motif, sc in same ch-3 sp and in next sc on First Motif, sc in each of next 10 sts, [sc in next ch-3 sp and in next sc on First Motif] twice, on working motif only, 3 sc in same ch-3 sp, join in first sc. Do not fasten off.

EDGING
Ch 1, working across long edge in each group of 16 sc of each motif, 4 hdc in same sc as joining, sk next sc, sl st in next sc, sk next sc, *4 hdc in next sc, sk next sc, sl st in next sc, sk next sc, rep from * around, join in first sc. Fasten off. *(176 [192, 208, 224, 240] hdc)*

Set aside.

BODICE

Notes: Cut a piece of elastic 21 [22, 23, 24, 25] inches long. Overlap ends ½ inch; sew together. Set aside. Bodice is worked in continuous rnds. Do not join unless specified; mark beg of rnds.

Rnd 1: Starting at top with pink, ch 90 [94, 98, 102, 106], being careful not to twist, join in first ch to form ring, ch 1, working over elastic, sc in each ch, forming casing. *(90 [94, 98, 102, 106] sc)*

Rnd 2: Sc in each sc around.

Rnds 3–5: Rep rnd 2. Remove marker at end of last rnd.

Rnd 6: Sl st in next sc, **ch 3** *(see Pattern Notes)*, dc in each sc around, working 50 **inc** *(see Special Stitches)* evenly sp around, join in 3rd ch of beg ch-3. *(140 [144, 148, 152, 156] dc)*

SKIRT

Rnd 1: Ch 1, sc in same st, sk next st, **V-st** *(see Special Stitches)* in next st, sk next st, *sc in next st, sk next st, V-st in next st, sk next st, rep from * around, join in first sc. *(35 [36, 37, 38, 39] V-sts, 35 [36, 37, 38, 39] sc)*

Rnd 2: **Beg V-st** *(see Special Stitches)* in same st, sc in ch-1 sp of next V-st, *V-st in next sc, sc in ch-1 sp of next V-st, rep from * around, join in 3rd ch of beg-ch 4. *(35 [36, 37, 38, 39] V-sts, 35 [36, 37, 38, 39] sc)*

Rnd 3: Ch 1, sc in next ch-1 sp, V-st in next sc, sc in next dc, V-st in next ch-1 sp, sc in next dc, V-st in next sc, *sc in next V-st, V-st in next sc, rep from * around. *(36 [37, 38, 39, 40] V-sts, 36 [37, 38, 39, 40] sc)*

Rnd 4: Rep rnd 2.

Rnds 5–12 [5–18, 5–24, 5–30, 5–36]: [Rep rnds 3 and 4] 4 [7, 10, 13, 16] times. *(40 [44, 48, 52, 56] V-sts, 40 [44, 48, 52, 56] sc at end of last rnd)*

Rnd 13 [19, 25, 31, 37]: Ch 1, sc in ch-1 sp of next V-st, V-st in next sc, *sc in ch-1 sp of next V-st, V-st in next sc, rep from * around, working

(sc in dc, V-st in ch-1 sp, sc in dc) in any 2 V-sts. *(42 [46, 50, 54, 58] V-sts, 42 [46, 50, 54, 58] sc)*

Rnd 14 [20, 26, 32, 38]: Rep rnd 4, working (sc in dc, V-st in ch-1 sp, sc in dc) in any 2 V-sts. *(44 [48, 52, 56, 60] V-sts, 44 [48, 52, 56, 60] sc)*

Rnd 15 [21, 27, 33, 39]: Ch 1, sc in ch-1 sp of next V-st, V-st in next sc, *sc in ch-1 sp of next V-st, V-st in next sc, rep from * around, join in first sc. *(44 [48, 52, 56, 60] V-sts, 44 [48, 52, 56, 60] sc)*

Rnd 16 [22, 28, 34, 40]: Beg-V-st in same sc as joining, sc in ch-1 sp of next V-st, *V-st in next sc, sc in ch-1 sp of next V-st, rep from * around, join in 3rd ch of beg-ch 4. *(44 [48, 52, 56, 60] V-sts, 44 [48, 52, 56, 60] sc)*

Rep last 2 rnds until piece measures 9½ [11, 12¼, 13¾, 15] inches from beg.

EDGING

Rnd 1: Ch 1, sc in same sc as joining, sc in each st and in each ch-1 sp around, join in sc. *(176 [192, 208, 224, 240] sc)*

Rnd 2: Ch 1, holding Border with WS facing and carefully matching sts, working through both thicknesses at same time, sc in each sc, join in first sc. Fasten off.

TOP EDGING

Hold piece with RS facing and foundation ch at top, join brown in any unused lp of foundation ch, ch 1, (sc, ch 2, sc) in same lp as joining, working in rem unused lps, sk next lp, *(sc, ch 2, sc) in next lp, sk next lp, rep from * around, join in first sc. *(90 [94, 98, 102, 106] sc, 45 [47, 49, 51, 53] ch-2 sps)*

STRAP
MAKE 2.

Row 1: With brown, ch 47 [50, 50, 50, 53], sc in 2nd ch from hook, sc in each rem ch across, turn. *(46 [49, 49, 49, 52] sc)*

Row 2: Ch 1, sc in each sc across, turn.

Rows 3 & 4: Rep row 2.

EDGING

Ch 1, (sc, ch 2, sc) in first sc, *sk next sc, sl st in next sc, (sc, ch 2, sc) in next sc, rep from * across, working across next side in ends of rows, work 3 sc evenly sp across, working across next side in unused lps of foundation ch, (sc, ch 2, sc) in first lp, **sk next lp, sl st in next lp, (sc, ch 2, sc) in next lp, rep from ** to first sc, join in first sc. Fasten off. (32 [34, 34, 34, 36] ch-2 sps)

FINISHING

Cut ⅜-inch-wide ribbon to length of each Strap plus 1 inch. Fold each end over ½ inch and sew to WS of ribbon to hide raw edge. With sewing needle and matching thread, sew ribbon to center front of each Strap to prevent stretching. Sew RS of bottom of one Strap ½ to 1 inch to WS of top of Dress. Do not sew other end of same strap at this time. In same manner, sew 2nd Strap to top, 4½ inches from first Strap. Lay dress flat and even out sides. Fold each Strap in half and place inside Dress so fold of Strap is 4½ [4½, 5, 5, 5¼] inches from row 1 of Bodice. Sew ends of Straps to WS of back of Dress. Beg and ending at center front, weave ¼-inch-wide ribbon through rnd 6 of Bodice going over 3 dc, under 1 dc. Tie ends in bow.

TOTE BAG
BORDER

Work First through 6th Motifs same as First through 6th Motifs of Dress, working rnd 1 with brown and rnds 2 and 3 with pink. Work 7th Motif same as last motif of Dress, working rnd 1 with brown and rnds 2 and 3 with pink.

EDGING

Rnd 1: Ch 1, sc in each of next 13 sc, sc in each of next 16 sc across next 6 motifs, sc in each of last 3 sc of first motif, join in first sc.

Rnd 2: Ch 1, sk same sc as joining, dc in next sc, working behind dc just made, sc in sk sc, *sk next sc, dc in next sc, working behind dc just made, sc in sk sc, rep from * around, join in first dc. Change to brown; cut pink.

Rnd 3: Ch 1, (sc, ch 2, sc) in same dc, sk next sc, *(sc, ch 2, sc) in next dc, sk next sc, rep from * around, join in first sc. Fasten off.

BASE

Rnd 1: With pink, ch 40, 5 sc in 2nd ch from hook (mark 2nd and 4th sc made), sc in each of next 37 chs, 5 sc in last ch (mark 2nd and 4th sc of last 5 sc made), working in unused lps on opposite side of foundation, sc in each of next 37 lps, join in first sc. (84 sc)

Rnd 2: Ch 1, sc in each sc around, working 3 sc in each marked sc, moving marker up to 2nd sc of each 3-sc group made, join in first sc. (90 sc)

Rnds 3 & 4: Rep rnd 2. (112 sc at end of last rnd)

Rnd 5: Ch 1, sc in each sc around, working 2 sc in each marked sc, join in first sc. (116 sc) Remove all markers.

Rnd 6: Ch 1, sk same sc, dc in next sc, working behind dc just made, sc in sk sc, *sk next sc, dc in next sc, working behind dc just made, sc in sk sc, rep from * around, join in first dc. Change to brown; cut pink. (56 dc, 56 sc)

BODY

Rnd 1: Ch 1, sc in each st around. (112 sc)

Rnd 2: Ch 1, sc in same sc as joining, sk next st, **V-st** (see Special Stitches) in next st, sk next st, *sc in next st, sk next st, V-st in next st, sk next st, rep from * around, join in first sc. (28 V-sts, 28 sc)

Rnd 3: **Beg-V-st** (see Special Stitches) in same st, sc in ch-1 sp of next V-st, *V-st in next sc, sc in ch-1 sp of next V-st, rep from * around, join in 3rd ch of beg-ch 4. (28 V-sts, 28 sc)

Rnd 4: Ch 1, sc in ch-1 sp of next V-st, V-st in next sc, *sc in ch-1 sp of next V-st, V-st in next sc, rep from * around, join in first sc.

Rep rnds 2 and 3 until piece measures 8 inches from rnd 1 of Body.

EDGING

Rnd 1: Ch 1, sc in same sc as joining, sc in each st and in each ch-1 sp around, join in first sc.

Rnd 2: Ch 1, holding Border with WS facing and carefully matching sts, working through both thicknesses **at same time**, sc in each sc across, join in first sc. Fasten off

BUTTON STRAP

Row 1: Hold Tote with RS facing, mark center 2 ch-2 sps from edging on either side, join brown in first of these 2 ch-2 sps, ch 1, (sc, ch 2, sc) in same ch-2 sp and in next ch-2 sp, turn. *(4 sc, 2 ch-2 sps)*

Row 2: Ch 1, (sc, ch 2, sc) in each ch-2 sp, turn.

Rows 3–19: Rep row 2.

Row 20: Ch 1, sc in first sc, ch 5 *(buttonhole made)*, sk next 2 sc, sc in next sc, turn.

Row 21: Ch 1, sc in first sc, 7 sc in next ch-5 sp, sc in last sc. Fasten off. *(9 sc)*

STRAP

Row 1: Hold Tote with RS facing, mark 3 ch-2 sps at side of Tote, join brown in first of these 3 ch-3 sps, ch 1, (sc, ch 2, sc) in same sp and in each of next 2 ch-2 sps, turn. *(6 sc, 3 ch-2 sps)*

Row 2: Ch 1, (sc, ch 2, sc) in each ch-2 sp across, turn.

Rep row 2 until piece measures 25 inches stretched. Fasten off.

INSIDE POCKET

Row 1: With pink, ch 18, sc in 2nd ch from hook, sc in each rem ch across, turn. *(17 sc)*

Row 2: Ch 1, sc in each sc across, turn.

Rows 3–15: Rep row 2.

EDGING

Ch 1, sc in each sc across, working across next side in ends of rows, sk first row, (sc, ch 2, sc) in next row, [sk next row, (sc, ch 2, sc) in next row] 7 times, working across next side in unused lps of foundation ch, sk first lp, [(sc, ch 2, sc) in next lp, sk next lp] 8 times, working across next side in ends of rows, (sc, ch 2, sc) in first row, sk next row, [(sc, ch 2, sc) in next row, sk next row] 7 times, join in first sc. Leaving long end for sewing, fasten off.

FINISHING

Sew end of Strap to 3 ch-2 sps opposite first side of Strap. Sew Pocket to inside of Tote on side of Button Strap below Motifs, taking care not to sew through to RS of Tote. ■

Rainbow Confections Apron

SKILL LEVEL

INTERMEDIATE

FINISHED SIZES
Girl's Apron: One size fits most
Doll's Apron: Fits 18-inch doll

FINISHED GARMENT SIZES
Girl's Apron: 17 inches wide x 21 inches long, excluding Neck Ties

MATERIALS
- Caron Spa light (light worsted) weight yarn (3 oz/251 yds/85g per skein)
  - 2 skeins #0014 rosalinda
  - 1 skein each #0013 dark driftwood, #0001 rose bisque, #0003 soft sunshine, #0005 ocean spray, #0006 berry frappe and #0007 naturally
- Size G/6/4mm crochet hook or size needed to obtain gauge
- Tapestry needle

GAUGE
19 sc = 4 inches; 18 sc rows = 3 inches

PATTERN NOTES
Weave in ends as work progresses.

Join with slip stitch as indicated unless otherwise stated.

Chain-2 at beginning of row counts as first half double crochet unless otherwise stated.

Chain-3 at beginning of row counts as first double crochet unless otherwise stated.

SPECIAL STITCH
Shell: 5 dc in st indicated.

INSTRUCTIONS
GIRL'S APRON
BIB

Row 1 (WS): Starting at top with size G hook and rosalinda, ch 24, sc in 2nd ch from hook, sc in each rem ch across, turn. *(23 sc)*

Row 2 (RS): Ch 1, 2 sc in first sc, sc in each sc across to last sc, 2 sc in last sc, turn. *(25 sc)*

Row 3: Ch 1, sc in each sc across, turn.

Row 4: Rep row 3.

Rows 5–16: [Rep rows 2–4] 4 times. *(33 sc at end of last row)*

Rows 17–22: [Rep rows 2 and 3] 3 times, **changing color** *(see Stitch Guide)* to dark driftwood in last sc of last row. *(39 sc at end of last row)*

Row 23: Rep row 2, changing to rose bisque in last sc. *(41 sc)*

Row 24: Rep row 3.

Row 25: Rep row 2, changing to dark driftwood in last sc. *(43 sc)*

Row 26: Rep row 3, changing to rosalinda in last sc.

Rows 27–30: [Rep rows 2 and 3] twice. *(47 sc at end of last row)*

Row 31: Ch 2, sc in 2nd ch from hook, sc in each rem sc across to last sc, 2 sc in last sc, turn. *(49 sc)*

Rows 32–42: Rep row 31, changing to dark driftwood in last sc at end of last row, turn. *(71 sc)*

WAISTBAND

Row 1: Ch 1, sc in each sc across, turn.

Rows 2–6: Rep row 1, changing to rosalinda in last sc at end of last row, turn.

SKIRT

Row 1: Ch 2 (see Pattern Notes), (dc, sc) in next sc, *sk next sc, (dc, sc) in next sc, rep from * across to last sc, hdc in last sc, turn. (35 dc, 35 sc, 2 hdc)

Row 2: Ch 2, *(dc, sc) in next sc, sk next dc, rep from * across to turning ch-2, hdc in 2nd ch of turning ch-2, turn.

Rep row 2 until piece measures 18 inches from top of Bib, ending with a RS row.

BOTTOM STRIPE

Row 1 (WS): Ch 2, *(dc, sc) in next sc, sk next dc, rep from * across to turning ch-2, hdc in 2nd ch of turning ch-2, changing to rose bisque, turn.

Row 2: Ch 2, *(dc, sc) in next sc, sk next dc, rep from * across to turning ch-2, hdc in 2nd ch of turning ch-2, turn.

Row 3: Rep row 2, changing to dark driftwood in last hdc, turn.

Row 4: Rep row 2, changing to rosalinda in last hdc, turn.

Rows 5 & 6: Rep row 2. At end of row 6, **do not turn.**

EDGING

Rnd 1 (RS): Ch 1, working across next side in ends of rows, work 55 sc evenly sp across to Waistband, sc in next 5 rows of Waistband, 2 sc in next row (mark last sc made as corner), sc in next 42 rows of Bib, working across next side in unused lps of foundation ch, 3 sc in first lp (mark 2nd sc as corner), sc in each of next 21 lps, 3 sc in last lp (mark 2nd sc as corner), working across next side in ends of rows, sc in next 42 rows of Bib, 2 sc in next row (mark first sc as corner), sc in each of next 5 rows of Waistband, continuing to work across side, work 56 sc evenly sp across to last row, working across last row, 3 sc in 3rd ch of beg ch-3 (mark 2nd sc as corner), sc in each of next 70 sts, 3 sc in last hdc (mark 2nd sc as corner), join in first sc. (312 sc)

Rnd 2: Ch 1, sc in each sc around, working 3 sc in each of 6 marked corner sc, moving marker up to 2nd sc of each 3-sc group and changing to dark driftwood at end of rnd. (324 sc)

Rnd 3: Ch 1, sc in each sc around, working 5 sc in each marked sc, join in first sc. Change to naturally; cut dark driftwood. (348 sc) Remove markers.

Rnd 4: Ch 1, sc in same sc as joining, sk next 2 sc, **shell** (see Special Stitch) in next sc, sk next 2 sc, *sc in next sc, sk next 2 sc, shell in next sc, sk next 2 sc, rep from * around, join in first sc. Fasten off. (58 shells, 58 sc)

POCKET
MAKE 2.

Row 1 (WS): With naturally, ch 12, sc in 2nd ch from hook, sc in each rem ch across, turn. (11 sc)

Row 2 (RS): Ch 1, sc in each sc across, turn.

Rows 3–17: Rep row 2.

Row 18: Ch 1, sc in each sc across. **Do not turn.**

EDGING

Rnd 1: Ch 1, working across next side in ends of rows, work 17 sc across side, working across next side in unused lps of foundation ch, 3 sc in first unused lp, sc in each of next 9 unused lps, 3 sc in last unused lp, working across next side in ends of rows, work 17 sc across side, working across row 18, sl st loosely in each of next 11 sc, join in first sc. (60 sts)

Rnd 2: Ch 3 (see Pattern Notes), 2 dc in same sc as joining, sk next 2 sc, sc in next sc, [sk next 2 sc, shell in next sc, sk next 2 sc, sc in next sc] twice, sk next 2 sc, 9 dc in next sc, sk next 2 sc, sc in next sc, sk next 2 sc, shell in next sc, sk next 2 sc, sc in next sc, sk next 2 sc, 9 dc in next sc, sk next 2 sc, sc in next sc, [sk next 2 sc, shell in next sc, sk next 2 sc, sc in next sc] twice, sk next 2 sc, 2 dc in last sc, ch 3, working in **back lps** (see Stitch Guide), sl st in each sl st across, sl st in each ch of beg ch-3. (5 shells, 23 dc, 8 sc, 14 sl sts, 1 ch-3 sp)

Rnd 3: Ch 1, sc in same ch as last sl st made, sk next 2 dc, shell in next sc, [sk next 2 dc, sl st in next dc, sk next 2 dc, shell in next sc] twice, sk next dc, sl st in next dc, sk next 2 dc, 9 dc in next dc, sk next 2 dc, sl st in next dc, sk next dc, shell in next sc, sk next 2 dc, sl st in next dc, sk next 2 dc, shell in next sc, sk next dc, sl st in next dc, sk next 2 dc, 9 dc in next dc, sk next 2 dc, sl st in next dc, sk next dc, shell in next sc, [sk next 2 dc, sl st in next dc, sk next 2 dc, shell in next sc] twice, sk next 2 dc, sc in first ch of next ch-3. Fasten off. *(7 shells, 18 dc, 2 sc, 9 sl sts)*

WAIST TIE
MAKE 2.
Row 1: With rosalinda, ch 119, sc in 2nd ch from hook, sc in each rem ch across, turn. *(118 sc)*

Row 2: Ch 1, sc in each sc across, turn.

Rows 3–6: Rep row 2. Fasten off at end of last row.

NECK TIE
MAKE 2.
Row 1: With rosalinda, ch 96, sc in 2nd ch from hook, sc in each rem ch across, turn. *(95 sc)*

Row 2: Ch 1, sc in each sc across, turn.

Row 3: Ch 1, sc in each sc across. Fasten off.

RAINBOW
Row 1 (RS): With dark driftwood, ch 25, sc in 2nd ch from hook, sc in each of next 3 chs, [2 sc in next ch, sc in each of next 4 chs] 4 times, changing to berry frappe in last sc, turn. *(28 sc)*

Row 2: Ch 1, sc in each of first 5 sc, [2 sc in next sc, sc in each of next 5 sc] 3 times, 2 sc in next sc, sc in each of last 4 sc, turn. *(32 sc)*

Row 3: Ch 1, sc in each sc across, changing to dark driftwood in last sc, turn.

Row 4: Ch 1, sc in each sc across, changing to ocean spray in last sc, turn.

Row 5: Ch 1, sc in each of first 5 sc, 2 sc in next sc, [sc in each of next 6 sc, 2 sc in next sc] 3 times, sc in each of last 5 sc. *(36 sc)*

Row 6: Ch 1, sc in each of first 2 sc, [sc in each of next 3 sc, 2 sc in next sc] 8 times, sc in each of last 2 sc, changing to dark driftwood in last sc, turn. *(44 sc)*

Row 7: Ch 1, sc in each of first 4 sc, 2 sc in next sc, [sc in each of next 4 sc, 2 sc in next sc] 7 times, sc in each of last 4 sc, changing to soft sunshine in last sc, turn. *(52 sc)*

Row 8: Ch 1, sc in each of first 3 sc, 2 sc in next sc, sc in each of next 4 sc, *sc in each of next 3 sc, 2 sc in next sc, [sc in each of next 6 sc, 2 sc in next sc] twice, sc in each of next 4 sc, rep from * once, turn. *(58 sc)*

Row 9: Ch 1, sc in each sc across, changing to dark driftwood in last sc.

Row 10: Rep row 9, changing to rose bisque in last sc.

Row 11: Ch 1, sc in each sc across, turn.

Row 12: Ch 1, sc in each sc across, changing to dark driftwood in last sc, turn.

EDGING
Rnd 1: Ch 1, 3 sc in first sc, sc in each sc across to last sc, 3 sc in last sc, working in ends of rows across next side, sc in each row to last row, 3 sc in last row, working across next side in unused lps of foundation ch, sl st in each lp, working across next side in ends of rows, 3 sc in first row, sc in each row across to beg sc, join in beg sc. Fasten off.

FINISHING
Sew 1 Waist Tie to RS of each edge of Waistband. Sew 1 Neck Tie to WS of each top corner of Bib.

Referring to photo for placement, sew Rainbow and Pockets to Apron.

DOLL'S APRON
BIB

Row 1 (WS): With rosalinda, ch 8, sc in 2nd ch from hook, sc in each rem ch across, turn. *(7 sc)*

Row 2 (RS): Ch 1, 2 sc in first sc, sc in each sc across to last sc, 2 sc in last sc, turn. *(9 sc)*

Row 3: Ch 1, sc in each sc across, turn.

Row 4: Rep row 2. *(11 sc)*

Rows 5–8: [Rep rows 3 and 4] twice, changing to dark driftwood at end of row. *(15 sc)*

Row 9: Rep row 3, changing to rose bisque at end of row.

Row 10: Rep row 2, changing to dark driftwood at end of row. *(17 sc)*

Row 11: Rep row 3, changing to rosalinda at end of row.

Row 12: Ch 2, sc in 2nd ch from hook, sc in each sc across to last sc, 2 sc in last sc. *(19 sc)*

Rows 13–15: Rep row 12, changing to dark driftwood at end of last row. *(25 sc)*

WAISTBAND

Row 1: Ch 1, sc in each sc across, turn.

Row 2: Ch 1, sc in each sc across, changing to rosalinda in last sc, turn.

SKIRT

Row 1: Ch 2 *(see Pattern Notes)*, (dc, sc) in next sc, *sk next sc, (dc, sc) in next sc, rep from * across to last sc, hdc in last sc, turn. *(12 dc, 12 sc, 2 hdc)*

Row 2: Ch 2, *(dc, sc) in next sc, sk next dc, rep from * across to beg ch-2, hdc in 2nd ch of beg ch-2, turn. *(12 dc, 12 sc, 2 hdc)*

Rows 3–10: Rep row 2, changing to dark driftwood at end of last row.

Row 11: Rep row 2, changing to rose bisque at end of last row.

Row 12: Rep row 2, changing to dark driftwood at end of last row.

Row 13: Rep row 2, changing to rosalinda at end of last row.

Row 14: Rep row 2. **Do not turn.**

EDGING

Rnd 1 (RS): Ch 1, working across next side in ends of rows, work 20 sc evenly sp across to Waistband, sc in next row, 3 sc in next row *(mark 2nd sc as corner)*, sc in each of next 15 rows of Bib, working across next side in unused lps of foundation ch, 3 sc in first lp *(mark 2nd sc as corner)*, sc in each of next 5 lps, 3 sc in last lp *(mark 2nd sc as corner)*, working across next side in ends of rows, sc in each of next 15 rows of Bib, sc in next row, 3 sc in next row *(mark 2nd sc as corner)*, continuing to work across side, work 21 sc evenly sp to row 6, 3 sc in 3rd ch of beg ch-3 of row 6 *(mark 2nd sc as corner)*, sc in each of next 24 sts, 3 sc in last hdc *(mark 2nd sc as corner)*, join in beg sc. Change to dark driftwood; cut rosalinda. *(120 sc)*

Rnd 2: Ch 1, sc in each sc, working 5 sc in each of 6 marked corner sc, join in first sc. Fasten off. *(144 sc)*

Rnd 3: Hold piece with RS facing, join naturally in any sc, sk next sc, 4 hdc in next sc, sk next sc, *sl st in next sc, sk next sc, 4 hdc in next sc, sk next sc, rep from * around, join in same st as joining of rnd 2. Fasten off. *(144 hdc, 36 sl sts)*

RAINBOW

Row 1: With dark driftwood, ch 13, sc in 2nd ch from hook, sc in next ch, 2 sc in next ch, [sc in each of next 2 chs, 2 sc in next ch] twice, sc in each of last 3 sc, changing to berry frappe in last sc, turn. *(15 sc)*

Row 2: Ch 1, sc in first sc, 2 sc in next sc, [sc in each of next 2 sc, 2 sc in next sc] 3 times, sc in each of last 4 sc, changing to dark driftwood in last sc, turn. *(19 sc)*

Row 3: Ch 1, sc in first sc, 2 sc in next sc, [sc in each of next 2 sc, 2 sc in next sc] 4 times, sc in each of last 5 sc, changing to ocean spray in last sc, turn. *(24 sc)*

Row 4: Ch 1, sc in first sc, 2 sc in next sc, [sc in each of next 2 sc, 2 sc in next sc] 6 times, sc in each of last 5 sc, changing to dark driftwood in last sc, turn. *(31 sc)*

Row 6: Ch 1, sc in first sc, 2 sc in next sc, [sc in each of next 2 sc, 2 sc in next sc] 8 times, sc in each of last 5 sc, changing to soft sunshine in last sc, turn. *(39 sc)*

Row 7: Ch 1, sc in each sc across, changing to dark driftwood in last sc, turn.

Row 8: Rep row 7, changing to rose bisque in last sc.

Row 9: Rep row 7, changing to dark driftwood in last sc.

EDGING

Ch 1, 3 sc in first sc, sc in each sc across to last sc, 3 sc in last sc, working across next side in ends of rows, sc in each row to last row, 3 sc in last row, working across next side in unused lps of foundation ch, sl st in each lp across, working across next side in ends of rows, 3 sc in first row, sc in each rem row across, join in first sc. Fasten off.

POCKET
MAKE 2.

Row 1 (WS): With naturally, ch 8, sc in 2nd ch from hook, sc in each rem ch across, turn. *(7 sc)*

Row 2 (RS): Ch 1, sc in each sc across, turn.

Rows 3–6: Rep row 2. At end of last row, **do not turn.**

EDGING

Rnd 1: Ch 1, working across next side in ends of rows, sc in each of next 6 rows, working across next side in unused lps of foundation ch, 5 sc in first lp, sc in each of next 2 lps, 2 sc in next lp, sc in each of next 2 lps, 5 sc in last lp, working across next side in ends of rows, sc in each of next 5 rows, 2 sc in last row, working in **back lps** *(see Stitch Guide)*, sl st in each st across to first sc, join in first sc. *(29 sc)*

Rnd 2: Ch 1, sc in same sc as joining, sk next sc, 4 hdc in next sc, sk next sc, [sl st in next sc, sk next sc, 4 hdc in next sc, sk next sc] 6 times, sc in last sc. Fasten off.

WAIST TIE
MAKE 2.

Row 1: With dark driftwood, ch 74, sc in 2nd ch from hook, sc in each rem ch across, turn. *(73 sc)*

Row 2: Ch 1, sc in each st across. Fasten off.

NECK TIE
MAKE 2.

With dark driftwood, ch 67, sc in 2nd ch from hook, sc in each rem ch across. Fasten off. *(66 sc)*

FINISHING

Sew 1 Waist Tie to RS of each edge of Waistband. Sew 1 Neck Tie to WS of each top corner of Bib.

Referring to photo for placement, sew Rainbow and Pockets to Apron. ∎

STITCH GUIDE

FOR MORE COMPLETE INFORMATION,
VISIT **ANNIESCATALOG.COM/STITCHGUIDE**

STITCH ABBREVIATIONS

beg	begin/begins/beginning
bpdc	back post double crochet
bpsc	back post single crochet
bptr	back post treble crochet
CC	contrasting color
ch(s)	chain(s)
ch-	refers to chain or space previously made (i.e., ch-1 space)
ch sp(s)	chain space(s)
cl(s)	cluster(s)
cm	centimeter(s)
dc	double crochet (singular/plural)
dc dec	double crochet 2 or more stitches together, as indicated
dec	decrease/decreases/decreasing
dtr	double treble crochet
ext	extended
fpdc	front post double crochet
fpsc	front post single crochet
fptr	front post treble crochet
g	gram(s)
hdc	half double crochet
hdc dec	half double crochet 2 or more stitches together, as indicated
inc	increase/increases/increasing
lp(s)	loop(s)
MC	main color
mm	millimeter(s)
oz	ounce(s)
pc	popcorn(s)
rem	remain/remains/remaining
rep(s)	repeat(s)
rnd(s)	round(s)
RS	right side
sc	single crochet (singular/plural)
sc dec	single crochet 2 or more stitches together, as indicated
sk	skip/skipped/skipping
sl st(s)	slip stitch(es)
sp(s)	space(s)/spaced
st(s)	stitch(es)
tog	together
tr	treble crochet
trtr	triple treble crochet
WS	wrong side
yd(s)	yard(s)
yo	yarn over

YARN CONVERSION

OUNCES TO GRAMS		GRAMS TO OUNCES	
1	28.4	25	⅞
2	56.7	40	1⅔
3	85.0	50	1¾
4	113.4	100	3½

UNITED STATES		UNITED KINGDOM
sl st (slip stitch)	=	sc (single crochet)
sc (single crochet)	=	dc (double crochet)
hdc (half double crochet)	=	htr (half treble crochet)
dc (double crochet)	=	tr (treble crochet)
tr (treble crochet)	=	dtr (double treble crochet)
dtr (double treble crochet)	=	ttr (triple treble crochet)
skip	=	miss

Single crochet decrease (sc dec): (Insert hook, yo, draw lp through) in each of the sts indicated, yo, draw through all lps on hook.

Example of 2-sc dec

Half double crochet decrease (hdc dec): (Yo, insert hook, yo, draw lp through) in each of the sts indicated, yo, draw through all lps on hook.

Example of 2-hdc dec

Reverse single crochet (reverse sc): Ch 1, sk first st, working from left to right, insert hook in next st from front to back, draw up lp on hook, yo, and draw through both lps on hook.

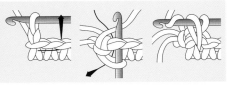

Chain (ch): Yo, pull through lp on hook.

Single crochet (sc): Insert hook in st, yo, pull through st, yo, pull through both lps on hook.

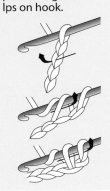

Double crochet (dc): Yo, insert hook in st, yo, pull through st, [yo, pull through 2 lps] twice.

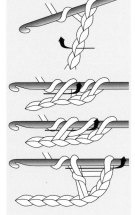

Double crochet decrease (dc dec): (Yo, insert hook, yo, draw lp through, yo, draw through 2 lps on hook) in each of the sts indicated, yo, draw through all lps on hook.

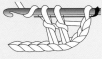

Example of 2-dc dec

Front loop (front lp) Back loop (back lp)

Front Loop   Back Loop

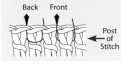

Front post stitch (fp): Back post stitch (bp): When working post st, insert hook from right to left around post of st on previous row.

Back   Front

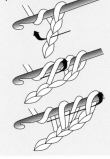

Post of Stitch

Half double crochet (hdc): Yo, insert hook in st, yo, pull through st, yo, pull through all 3 lps on hook.

Double treble crochet (dtr): Yo 3 times, insert hook in st, yo, pull through st, [yo, pull through 2 lps] 4 times.

Treble crochet decrease (tr dec): Holding back last lp of each st, tr in each of the sts indicated, yo, pull through all lps on hook.

Example of 2-tr dec

Slip stitch (sl st): Insert hook in st, pull through both lps on hook.

Chain color change (ch color change) Yo with new color, draw through last lp on hook.

Double crochet color change (dc color change) Drop first color, yo with new color, draw through last 2 lps of st.

Treble crochet (tr): Yo twice, insert hook in st, yo, pull through st, [yo, pull through 2 lps] 3 times.

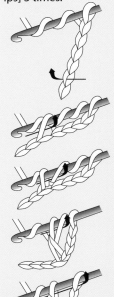

Metric Conversion Charts

METRIC CONVERSIONS

yards	x	.9144	=	metres (m)
yards	x	91.44	=	centimetres (cm)
inches	x	2.54	=	centimetres (cm)
inches	x	25.40	=	millimetres (mm)
inches	x	.0254	=	metres (m)

centimetres	x	.3937	=	inches
metres	x	1.0936	=	yards

INCHES INTO MILLIMETRES & CENTIMETRES (Rounded off slightly)

inches	mm	cm	inches	cm	inches	cm	inches	cm
1/8	3	0.3	5	12.5	21	53.5	38	96.5
1/4	6	0.6	5 1/2	14	22	56	39	99
3/8	10	1	6	15	23	58.5	40	101.5
1/2	13	1.3	7	18	24	61	41	104
5/8	15	1.5	8	20.5	25	63.5	42	106.5
3/4	20	2	9	23	26	66	43	109
7/8	22	2.2	10	25.5	27	68.5	44	112
1	25	2.5	11	28	28	71	45	114.5
1 1/4	32	3.2	12	30.5	29	73.5	46	117
1 1/2	38	3.8	13	33	30	76	47	119.5
1 3/4	45	4.5	14	35.5	31	79	48	122
2	50	5	15	38	32	81.5	49	124.5
2 1/2	65	6.5	16	40.5	33	84	50	127
3	75	7.5	17	43	34	86.5		
3 1/2	90	9	18	46	35	89		
4	100	10	19	48.5	36	91.5		
4 1/2	115	11.5	20	51	37	94		

KNITTING NEEDLES CONVERSION CHART

Canada/U.S.	0	1	2	3	4	5	6	7	8	9	10	10½	11	13	15
Metric (mm)	2	2¼	2¾	3¼	3½	3¾	4	4½	5	5½	6	6½	8	9	10

CROCHET HOOKS CONVERSION CHART

Canada/U.S.	1/B	2/C	3/D	4/E	5/F	6/G	8/H	9/I	10/J	10½/K	N
Metric (mm)	2.25	2.75	3.25	3.5	3.75	4.25	5	5.5	6	6.5	9.0

Annie's™ *Cute Crochet for Girls* is published by Annie's, 306 East Parr Road, Berne, IN 46711. Printed in USA. Copyright © 2012 DRG.
All rights reserved. This publication may not be reproduced in part or in whole without written permission from the publisher.

RETAIL STORES: If you would like to carry this pattern book or any other Annie's publication, visit AnniesWSL.com.

Every effort has been made to ensure that the instructions in this pattern book are complete and accurate. We cannot, however, take responsibility for human error, typographical mistakes or variations in individual work. Please visit AnniesCustomerCare.com to check for pattern updates.

ISBN: 978-1-59635-422-7
2 3 4 5 6 7 8 9